Old ABERFOYLE, THORNHILL and the FORTH VILLAGES

by
John Hood

The popularity of the Trossachs as a tourist destination owes much to Sir Walter Scott. Following the publication of *The Lady of Lake* in 1810 and *Rob Roy* seven years later, increasing numbers of visitors came to see the area in which the novels were set. Aberfoyle's Bailie Nicol Jarvie Hotel was only too happy to encourage such visitors and for almost 100 years they organised tours around the Trossachs. Passengers were conveyed in four-horse carriages accompanied by footmen dressed in red coats and grey top hats. Until 1932, when a new road was laid, the carriages used a private road owned by the Duke of Montrose. This took them over the Duke's Pass to Loch Katrine, where passengers could then embark on the steamer S.S. *Sir Walter Scott* for a cruise around the loch. With the opening of the new road, bus routes were opened up and eventually the carriages were withdrawn. Today, visitors to the area can sample a bit of (fairly recent) nostalgia by boarding the vintage 1950s' buses, the Trossachs Trundlers.

© John Hood, 2000
First published in the United Kingdom, 2000,
by Stenlake Publishing, Ochiltree Sawmill, The Lade,
Ochiltree, Ayrshire, KA18 2NX
Telephone / Fax: 01290 423114

ISBN 1 84033 110 0

THE PUBLISHERS REGRET THAT THEY CANNOT SUPPLY
COPIES OF ANY PICTURES FEATURED IN THIS BOOK.

The publishers wish to thank Hugh and Jessie McArthur for permission to reproduce the pictures in this book from their collection.

FURTHER READING

The books listed are a selection of those used by the author during his research. None of them are available from Stenlake Publishing. Those interested in finding out more are advised to contact their local bookshop or library.

Anon., *MacGregor's Guide to the Lake of Menteith and its Neighbourhood*, Eneas MacKay, 1900.
Bureau, Jack R., *Buchlyvie: A Village in Stirlingshire*, 1996.
Edwards, Alan A.B., *The Kippen Big Vine: The Story of the World's Largest Vine*, The Grape Press, 1991.
McCulloch, Stuart, J., *Thornhill and its Environs: A Social History*, Mungo Trust in association with Stirling District Libraries, 1995.
Rennie, R.C. (ed.), *The Third Statistical Account of Scotland: The County of Stirlingshire*, 1966.
New Statistical Account of Scotland Vol. 8, Dumbarton, Stirling, Clackmannan, 1845.

The 'Big Vine' at Forth Vineyards, Cauldhame, was at one time the largest vine in the world. The statistics are quite staggering. By 1910 the nineteen year old vine was already producing over 600 bunches of fine black grapes per year – more than London's Hampton Court Vine. By 1922 it had been officially recognised as the world's largest vine and was producing over 2,000 bunches. By 1960 it stretched over 300 feet through four large greenhouses and its main stem measured 55 inches in circumference. In total, it produced over 100,000 bunches of grapes in its lifetime.

INTRODUCTION

The villages of Aberfoyle, Arnprior, Buchlyvie, Gargunnock, Gartmore, Kippen, Port of Menteith and Thornhill lie in the Forth Valley between the Fintry Hills and the Menteith Hills. Together they encircle Flanders Moss, a broad and fertile marsh area.

The older villages, such as Gartmore and Gargunnock, were originally 'fermtouns' – settlements where most of the inhabitants made their living from the soil. In the eighteenth century so-called 'improving landlords' like Andrew Graham and Archibald Napier laid out new settlements at Buchlyvie and Thornhill. In this period the agricultural capacity of the area was further improved by the draining of large sections of Flanders Moss. Locals named the tenants in charge of these projects 'moss lairds'.

Besides farming, some villagers earned their living from passing trade as recognised drove roads ran through, or near, many of the villages and highland drovers would fatten their cattle on the land along the River Forth, on their way to lowland markets. One of the most famous figures associated with the area dealt in a different type of cattle trade, however, and there are many stories about Rob Roy MacGregor connected with the villages. In 1691, for example, the MacGregors raided every barn in the village of Kippen and stole all the villagers' livestock.

The area has always been more pastoral than industrial. However, in the 1700s weavers moved in, sometimes creating new settlements such as Low Town in Thornhill. Furthermore, many small cottage-type industries, such as tanning and basket-making, flourished in the area. Whisky and even wine were also produced in some of the villages.

Tourists have been coming to the area since the late 1700s and its popularity increased in the early 1800s with the publication of Scott's *Rob Roy* and *The Lady of the Lake*, both of which were set locally. The expansion of the railways in the 1800s, followed by the boom in car ownership from the 1950s, has allowed holidaymakers easy access to the villages and today the most successful local industry is tourism.

Lying to the east of Aberfoyle, Dounans Residential School Camp was established in 1939 by the Scottish Rural Housing Association to accommodate children evacuated from cities on Clydeside. After the Second World War the camp provided an opportunity for city children to undertake outdoor pursuits. Now called Dounans Centre, the camp is one of four in Scotland run by the Scottish Environmental and Outdoor Education Centres Association Ltd. The chalets in this photograph still stand, although No. 4 is now called 'Mentieth' and No. 5, 'Vennacher'.

This 1926 view shows the area of Aberfoyle's Main Street opposite the railway station and looks quite similar to the way it is today. One exception is the property between the Clachan Hotel and the turreted post office building. This housed the local Co-operative store, but was destroyed by fire. However, a modern purpose-built Co-op now stands in its place. Ironically, the area between this and the Clachan was once occupied by the local fire station (which actually adjoined the gable end of the hotel). At that time the fire wagons were all horse-drawn and evidence of three stables, and the hay loft above them, is still visible. The Clachan itself (once a temperance hotel) has undergone changes since this photograph was taken; for example, the bar now occupies one of the shops which flanked its entrance. These shops were originally a grocers and a sweetie shop, the latter being one of a small chain which had branches in many of the surrounding villages.

The Bailie Nicol Jarvie Hotel, 1938. This was built around the 1850s by the Duke of Montrose and takes its name from a character in the novel *Rob Roy*. For many years an image, purporting to be that of the Bailie, adorned the hotel sign. In addition, a replica coulter (part of a ploughshare blade which was used by Bailie Nicol Jarvie in his fight with the outlaw) used to hang from a tree in front of the hotel. The hotel ceased trading in the mid-1990s and the building has been converted into private housing. To right of the picture, in the distance, is the Bailie Nicol Jarvie Pavilion which was owned by the hotel.

The Bailie Nicol Jarvie Pavilion was a wooden structure erected as a tea room to cater for the ever-increasing number of visitors to Aberfoyle. Standing on Main Street, beside the railway station, it was certainly well-placed for customers. Today, the pavilion is now the premises of the Forth Inn and has been altered so much it is virtually unrecognisable. Indeed, other than the portion used as a ballroom, little of the original wooden structure remains. The area to the rear, once the site of the station, is now a car park.

The idea of a railway line linking Lennoxtown and Aberfoyle was first raised in 1861 by the Blane Valley Railway Company. A line was laid by the company in 1867, but unfortunately financial difficulties forced them to terminate this at Dumgoyne, far short of their intended target. Aberfoyle was eventually reached by a railway in October 1882 when the Strathendrick & Aberfoyle Railway Company extended the Blane Valley line to Buchlyvie and laid a branch line from there. This in effect meant that passengers undertaking the 34-mile journey from Aberfoyle to Glasgow had to travel on lines belonging to four different railway companies: Edinburgh & Glasgow, Blane Valley, Strathendrick & Aberfoyle and Forth & Clyde Junction!

Because of the proximity to the Trossachs and Port of Menteith, the station at Aberfoyle was used mainly by tourists. One way to see the area was to take a circular tour from Glasgow, visiting Aberfoyle, the Trossachs and Loch Lomond, using three modes of transport – train, coach and steamer. However, by the late 1920s the railway was losing passengers and, in a bid to cut costs and attract custom, a steam railcar named *Retaliator* was introduced on the Glasgow – Aberfoyle route. This special coach/train conveyed passengers from Aberfoyle to Blanefield, where they continued their journey to Glasgow by the normal steam train. Aberfoyle Station was demolished after the line was closed in 1959.

Until Aberfoyle merited a post office of its own, its mail was delivered to Doune. From there it was carried by a postman who had to walk all the way to Aberfoyle, delivering any other mail along the way. Once the postman's deliveries were completed, he would rest overnight in Aberfoyle, before setting off again the following morning on foot back to Doune with outgoing mail! In time Aberfoyle's population increased sufficiently for a post office to be established locally and by the 1930s it was located (on the right of the picture) beside Foresthill House, on the Loch Ard road. These properties remain more or less unchanged although the post office is now a private house named, not surprisingly, the Olde Post Office. The current post office is in the turreted building on Main Street which was erected in the 1880s.

Jean McAlpine's Inn, which is in the hamlet of Milton to the west of Aberfoyle, was once a popular hostelry and some of its trade would undoubtedly have come from the farmers who brought their grain for grinding in the old corn mill, which stood opposite. This was one of two mills in the Milton area; the other, which produced linen, closed down in the 1820s. The corn mill was in operation until 1917, and thereafter its water wheel was utilised by a threshing mill until 1923. The corn mill and the inn have both been preserved and form part of the Milton Conservation Area. The mill is now a private residence and Jean McAlpine's Inn functions as a tea room.

The estate of Gartmore dates from the beginning of the eighteenth century and was once the property of the Graham family, descendants of King Robert II. The village was laid out around the same time by the landowner, Nichol Graham, in order to enhance the estate and to house the estate workers. Although the village's original thatched roof cottages have now gone, most of the properties seen here at the turn of the twentieth century remain. An exception to this is James Davidson's bootmakers shop to the extreme right, which has been replaced by Laurel Cottage. The large villa adjacent to this but one is Terreran. Further up the hill on the left-hand side of the street is Gartmore Primary School. In the distance at the top of the hill is the Black Bull Hotel.

Black Bull Hotel, Gartmore

The Black Bull Hotel was established in the 1700s and besides catering for locals, benefited greatly from Gartmore's position on the drove road between Aberfoyle and Falkirk. With the demise of the droving trade, the hotel's custom came from tourism and, even today, it describes itself as being situated at the 'gateway to the Trossachs'. A few changes have been made to the exterior of the hotel since this photograph was taken: 'Black Bull' now replaces the name of Duncan Keir (the then owner) above the doorway facing the Square and the sign hanging from the gable end now advertises 'Belhaven Best'. In addition, the arched entrance in Main Street has had a porch added. In earlier times this part of the hotel had outside steps leading to the upper floor. Also removed was an old petrol pump which stood in front of the hotel on the Square.

Many of the properties in this view of Main Street remain today, including Wildenmore and Forth House on the extreme left of picture. Still on the left, in the distance, is Ochil View, which now houses the village store and post office. To the rear of this row of houses is the field where the local slaughterhouse once stood. The local 'midden' was also located in the same area. On the right, the small building with the cartwheel propped against its harled wall was originally the blacksmith's premises and is now Smithy House, a private residence.

Main Street, looking towards the entrance to Gartmore House, 1949. In the distance, on the left, is the junction with Station Road. Gartmore Station opened on the Strathendrick and Aberfoyle line in October 1882; it was demolished after the line closed in 1959. Today this view is not much changed, although there is no longer a telephone kiosk in front of what is now the Co-operative Store.

East End, Buchlyvie

The village of Buchlyvie was founded in 1680 by Sir Andrew Graham, an 'improving' landlord, and stands on the old military road running from Stirling to Dumbarton. To the left of this view of Main Street is the Buchlyvie Inn, built in 1851. Adjacent is the even older property of Old Spitalton which was erected in 1738. Beyond these properties is now the private dwelling house Arvain, which was formerly a plumber's yard. In the centre is Buchlyvie's war memorial and behind is the parish church, formerly South Church (so called to distinguish it from the North Church). This was erected in 1825 and was the first established church in Buchlyvie.

This early photograph of Main Street shows some of the older properties, now demolished, which stood near the present day junction with Station Road. The young lady is standing in the doorway of the Buchlyvie Inn, which was accessed via its railed 'bridge'. The two workmen would appear to be having a break from shovelling manure, their spades being propped up against the wall of the inn.

By 1850 Buchlyvie comprised of fifty-nine properties bordering both sides of Main Street, and in this view the full extent of it can be seen. Although the area to right of picture remains largely unchanged today, there have been significant changes on the opposite side of the street, in that a junction has now been created. In order to do this the properties just beyond the railings, including the Buchlyvie Inn, had to be demolished. Since this photograph was taken further properties in this middle section of Main Street have been demolished and replaced with modern housing.

Station Road, viewed from its junction with Main Street. The junction has been widened and the building on the left – once Cant's grocery store – is now a private house. Also, the low wall in front of this has been extended round the corner into Station Road and a pavement has been laid in front of it. Interestingly, the original road markings can still be seen today in the area between the house and the wall. The building on the right was demolished when the realignment work was done at the junction. Looking down Station Road, the long white building in the distance is the former United Presbyterian Church. This was established in 1740 when the minister at Kippen left the Established Church there and formed an Associate Congregation amongst his supporters in Buchlyvie, building this church at their own expense.

This photograph was taken at the junction of Main Street and Culbowie Road at the western end of the village. Some of the properties still remain, including the small white cottage to the extreme left and, in the centre, Wednesday Cottage which was built in 1871. Also still standing is the Public (or Memorial) Hall, with its four-faced clock tower capped by an ogee dome. The hall was built in 1884 at a cost of £1,234, paid for by public subscription. The tower is named after a local landowner, James Harvie of Ballockneck, who provided most of the money to build it. During the First World War the hall was used as a hospital for war-wounded servicemen. Unfortunately, it was badly damaged by fire in 1948 and had to be rebuilt. The property to right of the hall is Clifford Buildings. When it was demolished its red sandstone blocks were used as a base for the hall's car park.

Arnprior and its surrounding district has many associations with Rob Roy and this may account for the message on this postcard, which asserts that "Rob Roy is supposed to have stayed in this house" (although the house is not identified) and that the sender would give the recipient "the whole story" when next they met! In 1899 Arnprior consisted of no more than five cottages and these properties have mostly survived today. The cottage in the foreground at one time served as both a shop and post office, the latter being established in 1885; the 'hole-in-the-wall' post box still bears the initials 'G.R.' (George Rex), and a post office is still housed in this building, although in a different part. A bus shelter has now replaced the adjacent cottage, but the villa in the distance, Kep Cottage, is still standing. Today new properties fill the gap between this and the school further up the road.

Built in 1875, the school at Arnprior was, for a period, one of seven in Kippen Parish. It closed in the 1960s and the pupils were transferred to Buchlyvie Primary. Adjacent, to the left of the school, is the schoolmaster's house, at one time one of only two properties in Arnprior to have a water closet and a bath – such luxury! Today, both the school and schoolhouse are still standing and are largely unchanged, however, they now house The Furniture Shop and the Arnprior Nursery.

By the mid-1920s there were only three properties on the opposite side of the main road from the school. These were Easter Merkland, Middle Merkland and the old Arnprior Smiddy. The latter, seen here in the foreground, was at one time the only smiddy in the parish. This was operated by a single blacksmith who, in addition to his smithy work, also sold petrol. The smiddy is now the premises of cabinetmakers. The property beyond (which is the private house Arnfinlay) has been extended since this photograph was taken (coincidentally, this postcard was sent in 1968 to inform the recipient that from 19th August the sender's new address was Arnfinlay). The house in the far distance now has a garage alongside it.

Kippen's Main Street, looking towards Kippen Cross. Kippen originated as a farming community and was largely untouched by industrialisation, so much so that many of the older properties have survived. Of the buildings pictured, still standing is the Cross Keys Hotel on the left hand side of the road – just distinguishable by the sign above the door. Beyond the Cross is the property (now demolished) which at one time housed the old Crown Inn. Built in the eighteenth century, this building had crow-stepped gables and twelve-pane glazing. The properties to the right, which include the dwelling houses Craignish and Cruachan, still remain, as do the shops. Presumably at the time this photograph was taken one of these was a butchers, as the gentleman standing at what appears to be a delivery cart is wearing a striped butcher's apron. Coincidentally, one of these shops is still a butcher's (Skinner), the others being the post office and McNiall's Country Store.

In this later view of Main Street we can see a dramatic change in the condition of the road surface, now tarmacadamed with some pavements laid. In contrast, the properties look basically the same, although the cottage on the left (which is now Dougall's shop) has had a dormer extension. The adjoining cottage now has an upper level. The 100 foot spire of Kippen United Free Church can be seen to the left. At the Cross itself the war memorial has been erected. Just beyond, at the rear of the crow-stepped Crown Inn, is all that remains of the old Established Church, built in 1691. Within its graveyard is buried Jean Kay, wife of Robin MacGregor, youngest son of Rob Roy. In order to gain her estate, Jean was abducted by Robin and forced into marriage, after which he held her prisoner. Although eventually released, she died a few months later of smallpox. In 1754, two years after her death, Robin MacGregor was executed for the crime.

Although most of the buildings in this view of the Cross remain today, some have had a change of use. For example, the shop to the extreme right – which once housed McFarlane's general store and confectioners – is now a private dwelling. Further along can be seen the spire of the United Free Church. This was built in 1878, at a cost of £2,500, as a replacement for the old Free Church at Burnside. Most of the money came from the then minister, the Rev. Patrick Muirhead. By the time this photograph was taken, the once tall spire of the church had become unstable and had been considerably shortened and topped by a cupola.

CROWN HOTEL AND PARISH CHURCH, KIPPEN.   A.5423.

The two most distinctive buildings in this 1937 photograph of Fore Road are the Crown Hotel and the parish church. The former dates from the 1800s and is now one of the village's two pubs. However, Kippen once had eight public houses – and this during a period of severe restrictions imposed by the Crown in order to reduce drunkenness! These applied only to villages south of the Highlands and apparently the villagers managed to persuade the authorities that Kippen was situated north of the Highland line and therefore was exempt from any prohibitions. The parish church was built in 1823 and designed by the architect William Stirling. An extension was added some five years later with local landscape artist, D.Y. Cameron, being involved in the design. The clock in the bell tower, which was installed in 1881, was built by local watchmakers, R. & J. Dougall. Since this photograph was taken, the garage to the right of the hotel has made way for the hotel's Huntsman Restaurant.

KIPPEN FROM CHURCH TOWER, LOOKING EAST.

The gentle sweep of the Fintry Hills, which lie to the south of Kippen, are clearly visible in this view from the bell tower of the parish church. Also shown are the properties on the upper part of Fore Road, approaching Main Street at the Cross. Most of these remain today. Immediately below the tower, to the right, is the Crown Hotel. On the other side of the street, in the centre, is Gillespie Memorial Hall. This was erected in memory of William Honeyman Gillespie by his wife and presented to the village in 1877.

Another view from the bell tower, this time to the north of the village, looking across Flanders Moss towards the Menteith Hills. Among the trees is a stretch of the old Stirling to Dumbarton military road, known locally as the Kippen Straights. Many of the properties seen here remain today. Immediately below the bell tower, on Fore Road, can be seen the roof of Hawthorn Cottage. Opposite this are the houses Duncairn, Tubbs and Beech Cottage, the latter with its distinctively roofed dormers. Beyond this is the village hall, which was erected in 1897. At one time part of this was used as a school. Later, it was bought by an anonymous benefactress and presented to the community.

The Kippen Reading and Recreation Rooms on Main Street were opened in 1906. Also known as the Institute, the building was gifted to the village by Stephen Mitchell of Boquhan. The reading room at one time housed a library while the recreation room was, amongst other things, the venue for the summer ice table-top competitions played between nearby villages for the Cayzer Cup. (Summer ice is played on a table with a shiny surface, where two little 'counters' are pushed with sticks towards a target.) The property was refurbished in 1992 with money provided from various sources, including the Gannochy Trust (a charitable trust based in Perth). Today the Institute still stands, although the reading room has long since closed and only a small part of the building is used for recreational purposes. The remainder is now private housing and has been renamed Forth View.

The station at Kippen was opened on the Forth & Clyde Junction line in May 1856. Standing a mile from Kippen on the old Thornhill Road, it suffered – in common with other stations on the line – from being located so far away from the village it was designed to serve. By the 1920s, the line and the station were facing competition from local bus operators and finally, in October 1934, both were closed. Remarkably, most of the buildings in this 1922 view have survived although nothing of the line remains. The main station building to the right of the level crossing gates is now a private residence (Station Cottage) and the signal box to the left stands in its grounds. The low Dutch roofed building on the other side of the Thornhill Road beyond the station buildings has also survived and now forms part of a property called The Tryst.

Today, Kippen also encompasses the former villages of Shirgarton and Cauldhame. The latter was at one time famous as the home of the world's largest vine – the 'Big Vine'. In this 1930s' view the entrance to the old Forth Vineyards can be seen in the distance, just beyond the parked car. Nowadays, the vineyard has gone and a new road, The Vinery, gives access to a modern housing development. Further housing has also replaced the small cottage to the left of picture. The properties on the right still remain and have not altered much in appearance. Shirgarton's local claim to fame is that it was the home of William McQueen, a local man who was responsible for promoting a scheme in 1898 to raise funds for the erection of paraffin oil lamps for the streets in all three villages.

In 1891 Duncan Buchanan (formerly head gardener at Culzean Castle in Ayrshire), in partnership with his cousin Willie, established a market garden and vineyard at Cauldhame to the west of Kippen, on land leased from an uncle. Initially, a dozen Gros Colmon vines were planted in their vineyard. Although all thrived, one in particular outgrew the others, so much so that within fifteen years the rest had to be uprooted to allow it more room for growth. By the 1920s the Buchanan's Forth Vineyards had become famous for growing the world's three largest vines and visitors were charged sixpence to view them. By the 1950s, the vineyards had become primarily a tourist attraction with over 20,000 visitors a year, but when put up for sale in 1963 no firms offers were received, despite the 'Big Vine' producing a record 3,249 bunches. The vineyard was then closed down and no evidence remains of this phenomenon.

The village of Thornhill, which began life as a 'fermtoun', was once noted for its numerous whisky stills and many public houses – at one time it had eight! However, the stills are long since gone and only two hostelries remain – the Crown and the Commercial, which is pictured here. Besides being used by travellers, the village's hostelries were frequented by soldiers using the old military road which passed through the village. This road had been built after the Jacobite Rebellion and Thornhill became the last recognised stopping place for the military before reaching the barracks in Stirling. Perhaps reflecting the owner's allegiance to king and country, the Commercial Hotel was originally called the Lion & Unicorn. It reverted back to this name in 1951 and the old bas-reliefs of a lion and a unicorn still remain on the frontage. However, the signage on the roof and the old gas lamp above the entrance are away and the hotel's car park has replaced the buildings behind the coach in the photograph.

THORNHILL MAIN STREET, LOOKING WEST

By 1914, when this postcard was issued, Thornhill had merged with the neighbouring village of Norrieston. The joined villages largely comprised of one long Main Street, containing single-storey whitewashed cottages as well as some two-storey properties. The cottages were built gable to gable, with a lane between them every so often giving access to the long narrow sloping rear gardens. Rydal Cottage, the first property to left of picture, is typical of this style and, in common with the other cottages seen here, is largely unchanged today. The Commercial Hotel remains much the same as in the previous photograph. The outside pump further along from the hotel was one of a few used by the villagers for their water supply, which was drawn from a storage tank located near the North Common. The pumps were replaced in the 1940s by a piped supply from a local reservoir. Electric lighting was also introduced to the village at that time.

Main Street, Thornhill.

Further along Main Street and looking west, the view today is largely unchanged from this one taken around 1912, although a Spar store now replaces the Thornhill branch of D. & J. MacEwen's, the general merchants. Further along, on the left, is the Loan (formerly called Tam Dow's Loan after a local cobbler) which leads to the South Common. In the distance, the distinctive square tower of the Blairhoyle Masonic Lodge marks the site of the Cross. Beyond this, Main Road is known as The Hill. Just out of picture, to the right, is the Crown Inn. This dates from the 1790s and the old 'B' listed whitewashed stables to the rear are a reminder that once it was a staging post for coaches travelling between Stirling and Dumbarton.

The most prominent building at the Cross is the Blairhoyle Masonic Lodge. Reputedly designed by Rowand Anderson, this dates from 1893 and was said at one time to be the smallest Masonic lodge in Scotland. The square tower has a doocot, which is modelled on a similar one within the former Blairhoyle estate. The lodge and the other properties seen here remain largely unchanged, although the shop where the horse and cart are standing is now a dwelling house.

This photograph of John Robertson, alias 'Kippen Jock', was taken on the South Common. A local worthy, Jock, and his equally well-known donkey and cart, were once a familiar sight in Thornhill. Jock died at his home in Hill Street after he was kicked by a horse and is buried in nearby Norrieston Churchyard. At one time Thornhill had three commons, used by the villagers for grazing livestock. Attempts were made over the years by drovers and the many tinkers who stayed in the village (Thornhill was once known as 'Tinkertown'!) to use the commons, but these were stoutly resisted by the villagers. Today, there are two commons: North Common and South Common. The North has been preserved as it was while the South is much reduced in size and is used for recreational purposes.

The marshy South Common has also been known as 'the Bogs'. Parts of it were obviously firm enough for a game of football, although some of the boys might be barefooted to save their boots! During King George V's Silver Jubilee year in 1936 (some years after this picture was taken) the South Common was drained and part of it made into a children's play area. A permanent football pitch was also laid out at that time. A community centre has now been built on the Bogs and a new football pitch (still boggy) laid out beside it.

Tannaree was a stretch of the Aberfoyle road leading up to Thornhill Cross and was the site of a tannery which, at its peak, employed twenty people. The single-storey cottage in the foreground is the old smiddy, and the adjacent two-storey house was the tannery manager's house. The area beyond this is now occupied by a motor and tractor engineering works, while the house itself lies derelict and the smiddy has been replaced by modern housing. Formerly, Tannaree had been known as Shuttle Street, due to another local industry – weaving. In fact, it was weavers who, in 1701, established the area of the village known as Low Town and most of their cottages still stand. For many years Low Town was considered a separate community and had its own school and water supply. The school later became Thornhill Primary School. This was extended by an annexe in 1945 and is still in use today.

In a farming community the blacksmith would have held an important place in village life, being required for such things as shoeing horses and repairing farming implements. The smiddy at Tannaree seen here was one of two which served Thornhill over the years, the other being on Main Street. With the introduction of tractors and more sophisticated tools, the blacksmith's job became less significant and eventually the smiddies closed and the buildings were either demolished or used as dwelling houses. While this one was demolished, the one on Main Street survives as Corshill Cottage.

Main Street, Gargunnock. All the properties seen here have survived, except for the cluster of single and two-storey whitewashed houses in centre of picture. One of these was once the Model Lodging House and it is said that the tramps who frequented it would be "deloused and washed" before being fed. Another of the buildings was used as a post office until the 1960s. In the far distance, facing towards Main Street, is the White House which was formerly a public house. It is the oldest property in the Square and is reputed to be haunted. It is also said to have housed a school and a local basket-making business. These baskets, called oak spelk baskets, were made out of the branches of young oak trees. Gargunnock was the only place in Scotland where this particular type of basket was made and they were supplied to the likes of Coats, the Paisley thread manufacturer.

A 1920s' view of Main Street, looking west from the eighteenth century bridge at Bridgend. The conditions prevailing in the village at that time are clearly shown. On either side of the road, in front of the buildings, are the open street gutters, or 'sheughs', which had to be bridged to allow access to the properties. These sheughs (which were in use until the late 1950s, when underground pipes were laid) led to the Gargunnock Burn at the bottom of the hill. Although no street lighting is visible in this photograph, paraffin oil lamps were later used. The oil for them was paid for by the villagers with money raised from their annual ball, known locally as the Paraffin Ile (Oil) Ball. These oil lamps were replaced by gas lights in 1912 and, subsequently, electric lighting was introduced in 1945. At the time of this photograph, the road surface was rough and pavements had yet to be laid. Indeed, in 1936 the County Council refused to repair Main Street until the Gargunnock residents could prove that it was a public highway.

Guest House, Gargunnock.

Situated in the Square, Gargunnock Guest House was formerly one of the village's two public houses, the other being the nearby White House. Now a private residence called Trelawney Cottage, the Guest House's appearance has changed little in almost 100 years. Although not in the picture, it forms part of a row of buildings which includes Glenfoyle Cottage and McNair House. The former is so called because it was once the residence of the manager of nearby Glenfoyle Distillery. (This distillery – now demolished – was situated beside Dasherhead Farm and began production in 1826, ceasing in 1926.) These buildings, like so many in the Square, date from the eighteenth century and are all 'B' listed.

At the edge of the Square, where the foot of Main Street meets with Leckie Road, stands the Stevenson Memorial Fountain. Now disused, the fountain was presented to Gargunnock village in 1910 in memory of Jeannie Stevenson (née Miller) by her nephews. A fountain would seem a fitting tribute to Jeannie, whose son (local minister, the Rev. Robert Stevenson) had previously gifted Gargunnock its water supply. The two properties behind the fountain were later demolished, the one on the right being replaced by Burnside Cottage.

Station Road ran north towards Gargunnock Station, which has now been demolished. This station, on the Forth & Clyde Junction railway line, was the first stop on the route between Stirling and Balloch. Opened in 1856, it was primarily intended for industrial use, but in fact became little more than a rural line carrying passengers and local produce to the Stirling markets. Passengers could travel either first or third class and in 1900 a return to Stirling cost 1/6d for first and 1/0d for third. The line and station closed in October 1934. In this view of Station Road (taken at Burnside looking towards the Square) are two properties built in the 1950s by the County Council and, next to these, The Lea. All of these houses are virtually unchanged today, although a modern cottage now stands alongside The Lea. In the distance beyond the Square is the parish church, built in 1626. Gargunnock Burn runs under the small bridge in the foreground.

Public School, Gargunnock.

At one time Gargunnock was served by three schools, the earliest being the Parish School which opened in 1652. This was located at the top of Main Street in Carseview, a private dwelling house. The second, a church school, was opened in Ivy Dene in Main Street, and the third, a dame school (one usually run by an elderly mistress), was held for a period in the White House in the Square. The Parish School was replaced by the Public School in 1858. An annexe was added to it in 1911, just prior to this photograph being taken. Today, the Public School is now the Gargunnock Community Centre and the village children attend school in Kippen.

Opened to passengers on 26 May 1856, Port of Menteith Station was in fact sited much closer to Arnprior. It lay over three miles south of Port of Menteith and was the third stop on the Forth & Clyde Junction line. The name and location led to so much confusion that the Lake Hotel at Port of Menteith had to draw attention to this anomaly in their advertisements. The hotel also provided transport to and from the station for guests arriving by train. During the Second World War, the station was the dropping off point for ammunition due to be stored on Inchmahome Island on the Lake of Menteith and, while the ammunition was being transported to the War Department boats berthed on the lakeside, the road between the station and the lake became a 'restricted' area.

The Lake Hotel stands on the site of an earlier manse of the church which still stands next to the hotel. Formerly known as the Port of Menteith Inn, it was for many years the property of the Duke of Montrose. However, in 1936 the hotel, along with other family properties, was sold to help pay death duties. Since then it has had various owners and, although it has been extended since this photograph was taken in 1904, its appearance has not altered considerably.